C000258268

Good Advice
for a
Happy Life

Ariel Books

♦

**Andrews McMeel
Publishing**

Kansas City

ISBN: 0-7407-2277-8

Library of Congress Catalog Card Number: 2001096501

Introduction

"BE YOURSELF . . . DARE TO DREAM . . . remember to laugh"—we've all received advice over the years from family, friends, co-workers—even from our hairdressers and bartenders. Sometimes we nod our heads in casual agreement, but pay no more attention to the advice than we would to emptying the trash. At other times good advice arrives just when we need it most. Our best friend tells us to go on that job interview, and we get the job offer—and the happiness and fulfillment we're looking for.

Sometimes, like a thief, happiness sneaks up on us when we least expect it—and we are forever changed. We become open to new experiences; we feel that single ray of sunshine on a cold, wintry day; we feel blessed to be alive. At other times happiness can be not only hard to obtain but also hard to recognize. The search for happiness can be a lifelong process of discovery and trial and error. This thoughtful volume will help you discover what you can do to enjoy the peace and satisfaction of a happy life.

Life is a great big canvas;
throw all the paint
on it you can.

~~~~~

DANNY KAYE

I am somebody. *I* am me.
I like being me. And *I*
need nobody to make me
somebody.

LOUIS L'AMOUR

The greatest thing in the world is to know how to belong to oneself.

MONTAIGNE

Little deeds of kindness,
Little words of love,
Help to make earth happy
Like the heaven above.

JULIA FLETCHER CARNEY

To achieve, you need thought. . . . You have to know what you are doing and that's real power.

AYN RAND

. . . there is no end to what
you can accomplish if you
don't care who
gets the credit.

FLORENCE LUSCOMB

. . . some of us just go along . . . until

that marvelous day people stop intimi-

dating us—or should I say we refuse to

let them intimidate us?

~ *Peggy Lee* ~

To love abundantly is to live
abundantly, and to love
forever is to live forever.

~

Anonymous

He that is of a merry heart
hath a continual feast.

~

Proverbs 15:15

If you refuse to accept anything but the best, you'll get the best. Begin to live as you wish to live.

—

ANONYMOUS

For Life is the mirror

of king and slave.

'Tis just what you are and do;

Then give to the world the best you have,

And the best will come back to you.

Madeline S. Bridges

To be happy in this world, especially when youth is past, it is necessary to feel oneself not merely an isolated individual whose day will soon be over, but part of the stream of life flowing on from the first germ to the remote and unknown future.

~ *Bertrand Russell* ~

Find expression for a sorrow, and it will become dear to you. Find expression for a joy, and you will intensify its ecstasy.

~

OSCAR WILDE

None of us suddenly becomes something overnight. The preparations have been in the making for a lifetime.

❧

GAIL GODWIN

It is better to deserve honors and not have them than to have them and not deserve them.

MARK TWAIN

*L*aughing stirs up the blood, expands the chest, electrifies the nerves, clears away the cobwebs from the brain, and gives the whole system a cleansing rehabilitation.

Anonymous

Walk away from it until you're stronger. All your problems will be there when you get back, but you'll be better able to cope.

L<small>ADY</small> B<small>IRD</small> J<small>OHNSON</small>

If you can alter things,
alter them. *If* you cannot,
put up with them.

*E*NGLISH PROVERB

An effort made for the happiness of others lifts above ourselves.

LYDIA M. CHILD

*Love is a mutual self-giving
which ends in self-recovery.*

FULTON SHEEN

*I*f I were asked to give what I consider the single most useful bit of advice for all humanity, it would be this: Expect trouble as an inevitable part of life, and when it comes, hold your head high, look it squarely in the eye and say, "I will be bigger than you. You cannot defeat me." Then repeat to yourself the most comforting of all words, "This too shall pass." Maintaining self-respect in the face of a devastating experience is of prime importance.

Ann Landers

Those who don't know how to weep with their whole heart, don't know how to laugh either.

GOLDA MEIR

When you betray some-body else, you also betray yourself.

ISAAC BASHEVIS SINGER

*It is not our exalted
feelings, it is our sentiments
that build the necessary
home.*

⌒

ELIZABETH BOWEN

I still want to do my work, I still want to do my livingness. And I have lived. I have been fulfilled. I recognized what I had, and I never sold it short. And I ain't through yet!

~ *Louise Nevelson* ~

Love your country. Don't be afraid to stick your neck out. And take a chance on the young.

~

JACOB K. JAVITS

Life isn't a matter of
milestones but of moments.

⌒

ROSE FITZGERALD KENNEDY

$\mathcal{T}$here are nine requisites for contented living: health enough to make work a pleasure; wealth enough to support your needs; strength to battle with difficulties and overcome them; grace enough to confess your sins and forsake them; patience enough to toil until some good is accomplished; charity enough to see some good in your neighbor; love enough to move you to be useful and helpful to others; faith enough to make real the things of God; hope enough to remove all anxious fears concerning the future.

J. W. von Goethe

. . . often our bad moments are self-propelled. . . . And the drama is almost exclusively within our heads and hearts.

—

KATHLEEN TYNAN

*Lay aside life-harming
heaviness
And entertain a cheerful
disposition.*

～

WILLIAM SHAKESPEARE
KING RICHARD II

f I can stop one heart from breaking,

I shall not live in vain:

If I can ease one life the aching,

Or cool one pain,

Or help one fainting robin

Unto his nest again,

I shall not live in vain.

~~

Emily Dickinson

*T*hink enthusiastically about everything; but especially about your job. If you do, you'll put a touch of glory in your life. If you love your job with enthusiasm, you'll shake it to pieces. You'll love it into greatness, you'll upgrade it, you'll fill it with prestige and power.

Norman Vincent Peale

There is nothing to fear except the persistent refusal to find out the truth, the persistent refusal to analyze the causes of happenings. Fear grows in darkness; if you think there's a bogeyman around, turn on the light.

Dorothy Thompson

When you come right down to it, the secret of having it all is loving it all.

Dr. Joyce Brothers

. . . as one goes through life one learns that if you don't paddle your own canoe, you don't move.

KATHARINE HEPBURN

Never lose a chance of saying a kind word.

WILLIAM MAKEPEACE
THACKERAY

*To be happy is only to have
freed one's soul from the
unrest of unhappiness.*

~

MAETERLINCK

To have meaningful work is a tremendous happiness.

RITA MAE BROWN

Rule Number 1 is, don't sweat the small stuff. Rule Number 2 is, it's all small stuff. And if you can't fight and you can't flee, flow.

Dr. Robert S. Eliot

You never find yourself until you face the truth.

PEARL BAILEY

*H*appiness is good health
and a bad memory.

~

INGRID BERGMAN

*H*ere's what I taught my daughters:
Become women of substance. Work for
yourselves if you can. . . . And never,
never do a job if it isn't fun.

Carolyn See

UNIVERSITY PROFESSOR

Service to a just cause rewards the worker with more real happiness and satisfaction than any other venture of life.

CARRIE CHAPMAN CATT

. . . if you must leave a place that you have lived in and loved and where all your yesterdays are buried deep—leave it any way except a slow way, leave it the fastest way you can. Never turn back and never believe that an hour you remember is a better hour because it is dead. Passed years seem safe ones, vanquished ones, while the future lives in a cloud, formidable from a distance. The cloud clears as you enter it.

Beryl Markham

What really matters is what you do with what you have.

～

SHIRLEY LORD

Look to be treated by others as you have treated others.

~

PUBLILIUS SYRUS

$\mathcal{M}$any persons have a wrong idea of what constitutes true happiness. It is not attained through self-gratification but through fidelity to a worthy purpose.

~ *Helen Keller* ~

Light tomorrow with today.

ELIZABETH BARRETT BROWNING

In the end we will conserve only what we love. We will love only what we under-stand. We will understand only what we are taught.

~~~

SENEGALESE SAYING

*Never have a companion
who casts you in the shade.*

～

BALTASAR GRACIÁN

*H*appy the man, and happy he alone,

He, who can call today his own:

He who, secure within, can say,

Tomorrow do thy worst, for I have lived today.

~ *John Dryden* ~

Don't be afraid of the space between your dreams and reality. If you can dream it, you can make it so.

BELVA DAVIS

When you have faults, do not fear to abandon them.

CONFUCIUS

Stick with your family.

~

IDA P. SAFI

(ADVICE TO HER THREE SONS ON
HER DEATHBED)

Aim for success, not perfection. Never give up your right to be wrong, because then you will lose the ability to learn new things and move forward with your life. Remember that fear always lurks behind perfectionism.

Dr. David M. Burns

The future belongs to those who believe in the beauty of their dreams.

ELEANOR ROOSEVELT

*The best way to cheer
yourself up is to try to cheer
somebody else up.*

MARK TWAIN

$\mathcal{T}$his is the art of courage: to see things as they are and still believe that the victory lies not with those who avoid the bad, but those who taste, in living awareness, every drop of the good.

~ *Victoria Lincoln* ~

Giving whether it be of time, labor, affection, advice, gifts, or whatever, is one of life's greatest pleasures.

REBECCA RUSSELL

*P*ower is the ability to do
good things for others.

BROOKE ASTOR

The heart that loves is always young.

GREEK PROVERB

The true way to render ourselves happy is to love our duty and find in it our pleasure.

FRANÇOISE DE MOTTEVILLE

*Y*our heart often knows
things before your mind does.

POLLY ADLER

If you wish to succeed in life, make perseverance your bosom friend, experience your wise counselor, caution your elder brother, and hope your guardian genius.

~ *Joseph Addison* ~

Happiness lies in the absorption in some vocation which satisfies the soul.

SIR WILLIAM OSLER

*R*emember always that you have not
only the right to be an individual, you
have an obligation to be one. You cannot
make any useful contribution in life
unless you do this.

Eleanor Roosevelt

*I*f you don't eat at least one meal with your children, you give up your best opportunity to teach concern for the needs of others. Let's face it, chaotic meals contribute to self-oriented, pleasure-oriented values. The family meal is an excellent forum to learn about listening to others, taking turns, and, in general, constraining instinctual needs in a social context.

Dr. Lawrence J. Hatterer

*J*oy seems to me a step beyond happiness—happiness is a sort of atmosphere you can live in sometimes when you're lucky. Joy is a light that fills you with hope and faith and love.

Adela Rogers St. Johns

*O*ne is happy as a result of one's own efforts, once one knows the necessary ingredients of happiness—simple tastes, a certain degree of courage, self denial to a point, love of work, and, above all, a clear conscience. Happiness is no vague dream, of that I now feel certain.

George Sand

The love of life is necessary to the vigorous prosecution of any undertaking.

SAMUEL JOHNSON

For the happiest life, days should be rigorously planned, nights left open to chance.

MIGNON MCLAUGHLIN

$\mathcal{L}$et mystery have its place in you; do not be always turning up your whole soil with the ploughshare of self-examination, but leave a little fallow corner in your heart ready for any seed the winds may bring, and reserve a nook of shadow for the passing bird; keep a place in your heart for the unexpected guest, an altar for an unknown God.

Henri-Frédéric Amiel

I like living. I have sometimes been wildly, despairingly, acutely miserable, racked with sorrow, but through it all I still know quite certainly that just to be alive is a grand thing.

~ *Agatha Christie* ~

Asserting yourself while respecting others is a very good way to win respect yourself.

~~~~

JANICE LAROUCHE

*A*lways the rationalization is the same—
"Once this situation is remedied, then I will be
happy." But it never works that way in reality:
The goal is achieved, but the person who
reaches it is not the same person who dreamed
it. The goal was static, but the person's identity
was dynamic.

❧

Phillip Moffitt

*L*et the world know you as you are,
not as you think you should be—
because sooner or later, if you are
posing, you will forget the pose and
then where are you?

~ *Fanny Brice* ~

*Do noble things, do not
dream them all day long.*

CHARLES KINGSLEY

*To be happy, drop the words *if only* and substitute instead the words *next time*.*

SMILEY BLANTON, M.D.

*A*n individual's self-concept is the core of his personality. It affects every aspect of human behavior: the ability to learn, the capacity to grow and change, the choice of friends, mates, and careers. It is no exaggeration to say that a strong, positive self-image is the best possible preparation for success in life.

Dr. Joyce Brothers

. . . one of the goals of life is to try and be in
touch with one's most personal themes—
the values, ideas, styles, colors that are
the touchstones of one's own individual life,
its real texture and substance.

Gloria Vanderbilt

*P*ick battles big enough to matter, small enough to win.

JONATHAN KOZOL

*To be happy, we must not
be too concerned with others.*

ALBERT CAMUS

*H*appiness is the sense that one matters. Happiness is an abiding enthusiasm. Happiness is single-mindedness. Happiness is whole-heartedness. Happiness is a by-product. Happiness is faith.

Samuel M. Shoemaker

Give truth, and your gift

will be paid in kind,

And honor will honor meet;

And the smile which is sweet will surely find

A smile that is just as sweet.

Madeline S. Bridges

There is real magic in enthusiasm. It spells the difference between mediocrity and accomplishment. . . .

NORMAN VINCENT PEALE

The more passions and
desires one has, the more
ways one has of being happy.

~

CHARLOTTE-CATHERINE

*The delights of self-discovery
are always available.*

GAIL SHEEHY

*N*ever cease loving a person, and never give up hope for him, for even the prodigal son who had fallen most low, could still be saved; the bitterest enemy and also he who was your friend could again be your friend; love that has grown cold can kindle again.

Sören Kierkegaard

I naturally believe there will be a future, but I do not waste my time imagining its radiant beauty. . . . It seems to me that we ought to think first about the present. Even if the present is desperately dark, I do not wish to leave it. Will tomorrow be free from darkness? We'll talk about that tomorrow.

Lu Xun

To feel valued, to know, even if only once in a while, that you can do a job well is an absolutely marvelous feeling.

BARBARA WALTERS

*N*othing and everything cannot coexist. To believe in one is to deny the other. Fear is really nothing and love is everything. Whenever light enters darkness, the darkness is abolished.

~ *Helen Schucman* ~

Every day's a kick!

～

OPRAH WINFREY

Nothing great was ever achieved without enthusiasm.

RALPH WALDO EMERSON

$\mathcal{M}$oney is never to be squandered or spent ostentatiously. Some of the greatest people in history have lived lives of the greatest simplicity. Remember it's the you inside that counts. Money doesn't give you any license to relax. It gives an opportunity to use all your abilities, free of financial worries, to go forward, and to use your superior advantages and talents to help others.

Rose Fitzgerald Kennedy

*A*ll the world is searching for joy and happiness, but these cannot be purchased for any price in any marketplace, because they are virtues that come from within, and like rare jewels must be polished, for they shine brightest in the light of faith, and in the services of brotherly love.

Lucille R. Taylor

*N*othing in life is more exciting and
rewarding than the sudden flash of
insight that leaves you a changed
person—not only changed,
but for the better.

~Arthur Gordon~

I think success has no rules, but you can learn a lot from failure.

JEAN KERR

Focusing our attention—daily and hourly—not on what is wrong, but on what we love and value, allows us to participate in the birth of a better future, ushered in by the choices we make each and every day.

~ Carol Pearson ~

There is only one way to happiness and that is to cease worrying about things which are beyond the power of our will.

~

EPICTETUS

$\mathcal{Y}$es, I have doubted. I have wandered off the path. I have been lost. But I always returned. It is beyond the logic I seek. It is intuitive—an intrinsic, built-in sense of direction. I seem to find my way home. My faith has wavered but has saved me.

Helen Hayes

Anything you're good at contributes to happiness.

BERTRAND RUSSELL

The biggest human temptation is . . . to settle for too little.

~

THOMAS MERTON

Do not quench your inspiration and your imagination; do not become the slave of your model.

VINCENT VAN GOGH

Give me a sense of humor, Lord,

Give me the grace to see a joke,

To get some pleasure out of life

And pass it on to other folk.

Anonymous

The great man is he who does not lose his child's heart.

MENCIUS

$\mathcal{Y}$ou must learn day by day, year by year, to broaden your horizons. The more things you love, the more you are interested in, the more you enjoy, the more you are indignant about— the more you have left when anything happens.

Ethel Barrymore

Always look out for the sunlight the Lord sends into your days.

～

HOPE CAMPBELL

Make voyages. Attempt them. There's nothing else.

TENNESSEE WILLIAMS

Today well-lived . . . makes
every tomorrow a vision
of Hope.

~

ANONYMOUS

*N*o one can go it alone. Somewhere along the way is the person who gives you that job, who has faith that you can make it. And everyone has something to work with, if only he will look for it.

~ *Grace Gil Olivarez* ~

*I*n the time of your life, live—so that in that good time there shall be no ugliness or death for yourself or for any life your life touches. Seek goodness everywhere, and where it is found, bring it out of its hiding-place and let it be free and unashamed.

William Saroyan

*What you can't get out of,
get into wholeheartedly.*

MIGNON MCLAUGHLIN

*F*aith is an excitement and an enthusiasm; it is a condition of intellectual magnificence to which we must cling as to a treasure and not squander in . . . priggish argument.

~ *George Sand* ~

It is neither wealth nor splendor but tranquillity and occupation which give happiness.

THOMAS JEFFERSON

The only gracious way to accept an insult is to ignore it: if you can't ignore it, top it: if you can't top it, laugh at it: if you can't laugh at it, it's probably deserved.

~ *Russell Lynes* ~

Do not let people put you down. Believe in yourself and stand for yourself and trust yourself.

JACOB NEUSNER

Happiness or misfortune are prescribed by law of Heaven, but their source comes from ourselves.

~

NGUYEN DU

*L*ife can be wildly tragic at times, and I've had my share. But whatever happens to you, you have to keep a slightly comic attitude. In the final analysis, you have got not to forget to laugh.

~ *Katharine Hepburn* ~

*B*e glad today. Tomorrow may bring tears.

Be brave today. The darkest night will pass.

And golden rays will usher in the dawn.

Who conquers now shall rule the coming years.

Sarah Knowles Bolton

My motto——*sans limites.*

❦

ISADORA DUNCAN

Real joy comes not from ease or riches or from the praise of men, but from doing something worthwhile.

SIR WILFRED GRENFELL

*H*uman felicity is produc'd not so much by great pieces of good fortune that seldom happen, as by little advantages that occur every day.

Benjamin Franklin

*B*e substantially great in
thyself, and more than thou
appearest unto others.

SIR THOMAS BROWNE

Whoever is happy will make others happy too.

ANNE FRANK

*I*t has never been, and never will be easy work! But the road that is built in hope is more pleasant to the traveler than the road built in despair, even though they both lead to the same destination.

Marion Zimmer Bradley

. . . *joy runs deeper than despair.*

CORRIE TEN BOOM

Nobody holds a good opinion of a man who has a low opinion of himself.

ANTHONY TROLLOPE

If you are wise, be wise;
keep what goods the gods
provide you.

TITUS MACCIUS PLAUTUS

*H*appiness is equilibrium. Shift your weight. Equilibrium is pragmatic. You have to get everything into proportion. You compensate, rebalance yourself so that you maintain your angle to your world. When the world shifts, you shift.

Tom Stoppard

The trick to life, I can say now in my advanced age, is to stop trying to make it so important.

LORETTA YOUNG

You find yourself refreshed by the presence of cheerful people. Why not make an honest effort to confer that pleasure on others? Half the battle is gained if you never allow yourself to say anything gloomy.

Lydia M. Child

When we can't dream any longer, we die.

～

EMMA GOLDMAN

Our strength is often composed of the weaknesses we're damned if we're going to show.

~

MIGNON McLAUGHLIN

. . . we have a tendency to obscure the forest of simple joys with the trees of problems.

CHRISTIANE COLLANGE

*H*appiness is to take up the struggle in the midst of the raging storm and not to pluck the lute in the moonlight or recite poetry among the blossoms.

~ *Ding Lee* ~

Cheerfulness keeps up a kind of daylight in the mind, and fills it with a steady and perpetual serenity.

JOSEPH ADDISON

*I*f you cannot be happy in one way, be in another, and this felicity of disposition wants but little aid from philosophy, for health and good humor are almost the whole affair. Many run about after felicity, like an absent man hunting for his hat, while it is in his hand or on his head.

James Sharp

We are apt to mistake our vocation by looking out of the way for occasions to exercise great and rare virtues, and by stepping over the ordinary ones that lie directly in the road before us.

Hannah More

Better to have loved and
lost, than not to have loved
at all.

~

SENECA

If you ever find happiness by hunting for it, you will find it, as the old
woman did her lost spectacles, safe on
her own nose all the time.

~ *Josh Billings* ~

Life without idealism is
empty indeed. We just have
hope or starve to death.

PEARL S. BUCK

Seek not out the things that
are too hard for thee, neither
search the things that are
beyond thy strength.

~

*A*POCRYPHA

Two things are bad for the heart—running uphill and running down people.

BERNARD GIMBEL

Love is something like the clouds that were in the sky before the sun came out. You cannot touch the clouds, you know; but you feel the rain and know how glad the flowers and the thirsty earth are to have it after a hot day. You cannot touch love either; but you feel the sweetness that it pours into everything.

Annie Sullivan

I began to have an idea of my life, not as the slow shaping of achievement to fit my preconceived purposes, but as the gradual discovery and growth of a purpose which I did not know.

Joanna Field

Don't hurry, don't worry. You're only here for a short visit. So be sure to stop and smell the flowers.

WALTER HAGEN

*Take your work seriously,
but never yourself.*

❦

DAME MARGOT FONTEYN

Always leave something to wish for; otherwise you will be miserable from your very happiness.

❧

BALTASAR GRACIÁN

Creativity is inventing, experimenting, growing, taking risks, breaking rules, making mistakes, and having fun.

~

MARY LOU COOK

Be content with your lot;
one cannot be first in
everything.

~~~~~

*A*ESOP

I look on that man as happy, who, when there is question of success, looks into his work for a reply.

~~~

RALPH WALDO EMERSON

*I*t is for us to pray not for tasks
equal to our powers, but for powers
equal to our tasks, to go forward with a
great desire forever beating at the door
of our hearts as we travel towards
our distant goal.

~ *Helen Keller* ~

$\mathcal{B}$e not too critical of others,
and love much.

❧

Julia Huxley

(TO HER SON ALDOUS HUXLEY)

Man an needs, for his happiness, not only the enjoyment of this or that, but hope and enterprise and change.

BERTRAND RUSSELL

The moments of happiness we enjoy take us by surprise. It is not that we seize them, but that they seize us.

ASHLEY MONTAGU

*Life is what we make it,
always has been, always
will be.*

GRANDMA MOSES

There's only one thing in this world that's worth having. Love. L-o-v-e. You love somebody, somebody loves you. That's all there is to it.

Charles Mergendahl

The greatest assassin of life
is haste, the desire to reach
things before the right time
which means overreaching
them.

❧

JUAN RAMÓN JIMÉNEZ

*T*o live content with small means; to seek elegance rather than luxury, and refinement rather than fashion; to be worthy, not respectable, and wealthy, not rich; to study hard, think quietly, talk gently, act frankly; to listen to the stars and birds, to babes and sages, with open heart; to bear on cheerfully, do all bravely, awaiting occasions, worry never; in a word to, like the spiritual, unbidden and unconscious, grow up through the common.

William Ellery Channing

Happiness must be cultivated. It is like character. It is not a thing to be safely let alone for a moment, or it will run to weeds.

ELIZABETH STUART PHELPS

*There must be more to life
than having everything.*

~

MAURICE SENDAK

You have to believe in
happiness or happiness
never comes.

〜

DOUGLAS MALLOCH

If you give your life as a
wholehearted response to love,
then love will
wholeheartedly respond to you.

❦

MARIANNE WILLIAMSON

$\mathcal{T}$here are two things to aim at in life: first, to get what you want; and, after that, to enjoy it. Only the wisest of mankind achieve the second.

~ *Logan Pearsall Smith* ~

*L*et everyone try and find that as a result of daily prayer he adds something new to his life, something with which nothing can be compared.

Mohandas K. Gandhi

A man hath no better
thing under the sun, than to
eat, and to drink, and to
be merry.

~

*E*CCLESIASTES 8:15

Success is not a place at which one arrives but rather . . . the spirit with which one undertakes and continues the journey.

Alex Noble

. . . I finally figured out the only reason to be alive is to enjoy it.

~ *Rita Mae Brown* ~

Happiness is not a state to arrive at—but a manner of traveling.

MARGARET LEE RUNBECK

Hate cannot destroy hate, but love can and does. Not the soft and negative thing that has carried the name and misrepresented the emotion, but love that suffers all things and is kind, love that accepts responsibility, love that marches, love that suffers, love that bleeds and dies for a great cause—but to rise again.

Daniel A. Poling

There is no beyond, there is only here, the infinitely small, infinitely great and utterly demanding present.

IRIS MURDOCH

One of the oldest human
needs is having someone to
wonder where you are when
you don't come home
at night.

MARGARET MEAD

*A*n open mind, humility,
determination, enthusiasm, unselfish-
ness, plus a love of action (inspired
work) are the steps in a moving stairway
to the stars.

∾ *Melvin J. Evans* ∾

*L*ike water which can clearly mirror the sky and the trees only so long as its surface is undisturbed, the mind can only reflect the true image of the Self when it is tranquil and wholly relaxed.

Indra Devi

I had found a kind of serenity, a new maturity. . . . I didn't feel better or stronger than anyone else but it seemed no longer important whether everyone loved me or not—more important now was for me to love them. Feeling that way turns your whole life around; living becomes the act of giving. When I do a performance now, I still need and like the adulation of an audience, of course, but my *real* satisfaction comes from what I have given of myself, from the joyful act of singing itself.

Beverly Sills

My mother used to say, "Watch yourself. The higher you are, the farther you can fall. Never let pride be your guiding principle. Pride itself. Let your accomplishments speak for you."

~ *Morgan Freeman* ~

We can only learn to love
by loving.

Iris Murdock

Whatever games are played with us, we must play no games with ourselves, but deal in our privacy with the last honesty and truth.

RALPH WALDO EMERSON

*R*unning a business is not the important thing but making a commitment to do the whole job, making a commitment to improve things, to influence the world is. One of the most satisfying things is to help others to be creative, to take responsibility, to be challenged in their jobs.

Kenneth H. Olsen

$\mathcal{T}$he story of love is not important.
What is important is that one is capable
of love. It is perhaps the only glimpse
we are permitted of eternity.

~ *Helen Hayes* ~

Some problems are just too complicated for rational, logical solutions. They admit of insights, not answers.

JEROME WIESNER

I'm afraid I'm an incorrigible life-lover, life-wonderer, and adventurer.

EDITH WHARTON

*Peace means loyalty to self.
. . . And loyalty to one's
self means never a gap
between thought, speech, act.*

~

RUTH BEEBE HILL

It just ain't possible to explain some things. It's interesting to wonder on them and do some speculation, but the main thing is you have to accept it— take it for what it is, and get on with your growing.

 *Jim Dodge*

*K*now how to draw away. . . .
Do not belong so wholly to others
that you do not belong to yourself.
Neither be all, nor give all to anyone; neither
blood, nor friendship, nor the most pressing
obligation, justifies it, for there is a big difference
between the bestowal of your affection and the
bestowal of yourself.

Baltasar Gracián

Where there is great love
there are always miracles.

WILLA CATHER

You are unique, and if that is not fulfilled, then something has been lost.

MARTHA GRAHAM

*O*ur happiness depends on
wisdom all the way.

SOPHOCLES

*M*ay we never let the things we can't have, or don't have, or shouldn't have, spoil our enjoyment of the things we do have and can have. As we value our happiness let us not forget it, for one of the greatest lessons in life is learning to be happy without the things we cannot or should not have.

Richard L. Evans

*F*our goals for a meaningful life:

—seek out a need of the world

—work

—forget self

—trust God

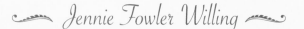 *Jennie Fowler Willing*

*E*ach person has his own safe place—
running, painting, swimming, fishing, weaving,
gardening. The activity itself is less important
than the act of drawing on your own
resources.

~

Barbara Gordon

*T*o be a leader you must feel that you

are both everything and nothing—

nothing in that you are on this earth for

a few years out of billions . . .

everything, because you are at the center

of all activity in your world.

~ *Edith Weiner* ~

$\mathcal{T}$he question is not whether you're frightened or not, but whether you or the fear is in control. If you say, "I won't be frightened," and then you experience fear, most likely you'll succumb to it, because you're paying attention to it. The correct thing to tell yourself is, "If I do get frightened, I will stay in command."

$\smile$ $\smile$ $\smile$

Dr. Herbert Fensterheim

A happy woman is one
who has no cares at all; a
cheerful woman is one who
has cares but doesn't let them
get her down.

~

BEVERLY SILLS

*Whoso loves
Believes the impossible.*

ELIZABETH BARRETT BROWNING

*N*ever feel self-pity, the most
destructive emotion there is. How awful
to be caught up in the terrible
squirrel cage of self.

Millicent Fenwick

'Tis easy enough to be pleasant, when life flows like a song. But the man worthwhile is the one who will smile when everything goes dead wrong.

Ella Wheeler Wilcox

*S*o long as we love, we serve. So long as we are loved by others, I would almost say we are indispensable; and no man is useless while he has a friend.

Robert Louis Stevenson

Remembering the past gives power to the present.

~

FAYE MYENNE NG

*Beware how you take away
hope from any human being.*

Dr. Oliver Wendell
Holmes

$\mathcal{L}$ove has nothing to do with what you are expecting to get—only what you are expecting to give—which is everything. What you will receive in return varies. But it really has no connection with what you give. You give because you love and cannot help giving. If you are very lucky, you may be loved back. That is delicious but it does not necessarily happen.

Katharine Hepburn

Resolve to be thyself:
and know, that he
Who finds himself,
loses his misery.

～

MATTHEW ARNOLD

*L*et us go singing as far as we go; the road will be less tedious.

*V*IRGIL

If you can't change your
fate, change your attitude.

~~~

AMY TAN

It's a beautiful world to see,
Or it's dismal in every zone,
The thing it must be
in its gloom or its gleam
Depends on yourself alone.

ANONYMOUS

*E*very production of genius must be

the production of enthusiasm.

~ *Benjamin Disraeli* ~

If you want to be happy,
be.

LEO TOLSTOY

*U*ntil you make peace with who you are, you'll never be content with what you have.

Doris Mortman

*W*hen met with opposition, even if it should be from your husband or your children, endeavour to overcome it by argument and not by authority, for a victory dependent on authority is unreal and illusory.

Bertrand Russell

If you wish to be loved,
show more of your faults than
your virtues.

EDWARD BULWER-LYTTON

Leave undone whatever you hesitate to do.

YOSHIDA KANKO

Love is the life of man.

EMANUEL SWEDENBORG

*T*he way to make yourself pleasing to others is to show that you care for them. . . . The seeds of love can never grow but under the warm and genial influence of kind feelings and affectionate manners.

William Wirt

(TO HIS DAUGHTER)

$\mathcal{L}$ife's what's important. Walking, houses, family. Birth and pain and joy. Acting's just waiting for a custard pie. That's all.

～～

Katharine Hepburn

*C*ontinuity gives us roots; change gives us branches, letting us stretch and grow and reach new heights.

Pauline R. Kezer

A man can succeed at
almost anything for which he
has unlimited enthusiasm.

⟋⟋ CHARLES *M.* SCHWAB ⟍⟍

*H*appiness, grief, gaiety, sadness, are by nature contagious. Bring your health and your strength to the weak and sickly, and so you will be of use to them. Give them, not your weakness, but your energy, so you will revive and lift them up. Life alone can rekindle life.

Henri-Frédéric Amiel

Fear . . . is forward. No one is afraid of yesterday.

~ RENATA ADLER ~

*It's the most unhappy
people who most fear change.*

~ MIGNON McLAUGHLIN ~

*T*he only good advice is a good example. You don't tell them a whole lot of anything. You show them by doing. You teach values by making choices in their presence. They see what you do and they make judgments on it.

Ossie Davis

*B*elieve all the good you can of everyone. Do not measure others by yourself. If they have advantages which you have not, let your liberality keep pace with their good fortune. Envy no one, and you need envy no one.

William Hazlitt

Behold, we live through all things,—famine, thirst,
Bereavement, pain; all grief and misery,
All woe and sorrow; life inflicts its worst
On soul and body,—but we cannot die,
Though we be sick, and tired, and tired,
and faint, and worn,
Lo, all things can be borne!

Elizabeth Akers Allen

We have all known the
long loneliness and we have
learned that the only solution
is love.

~

DOROTHY DAY

Love makes all hard hearts gentle.

GEORGE HERBERT

Life is not an easy thing to embrace, like

trying to hug an elephant. . .

~~~ Diane Wakoski ~~~

Nothing is interesting if you're not interested.

HELEN MAC INNESS

If you want to know the single most important insight I've learned in living my own life, it is the right understanding of happiness. The modern understanding of happiness is confused with pleasure or satisfaction, having a good time. Aristotle used the Greek word eudaimonia, and that translates into "good life." He meant the good life as a whole. But how can you experience the good life? What you can have is the moral aim of leading a whole good life—by building it the way one builds part of a play.

Mortimer Adler

*J*ump into the middle of things, get
your hands dirty, fall flat on your face,
and then reach for the stars.

Joan L. Curcio

If only we'd stop trying to
be happy we'd have a pretty
good time.

Edith Wharton

The hand that in life grips with a miser's clutch, and the ear that refuses to heed the pleading voice of humanity forfeit the most precious of all gifts of earth and of heaven— the happiness that comes of doing good to others.

Amos G. Carter

Happiness depends upon ourselves.

ARISTOTLE

$\mathcal{M}$ake no little plans. They have no
magic to stir men's blood. Make big
plans: aim high in hope and work.

Daniel Hudson Burnham

I think laughter may be a form of courage. . . . As humans we sometimes stand tall and look into the sun and laugh, and I think we are never more brave than when we do that.

Linda Ellerbee

*H*ave fun. I don't kid myself. Life is very

fragile, and success doesn't change that. If

anything, success makes it more fragile.

Anything can change, without warning, and

that's why I try not to take any of what's

happened too seriously.

Donald J. Trump

It's never too late—never too late to start over, never too late to be happy.

JANE FONDA

$\mathcal{T}$o me, the sea is like a person—like a child that I've known a long time. It sounds crazy, I know, but when I swim in the sea I talk to it. I never feel alone when I'm out there.

Gertrude Ederle

*O*ne ought every day at least to hear a little song, read a good poem, see a fine picture, and, if it were possible, to speak a few reasonable words.

J. W. von Goethe

*L*ove, like the opening of the heavens to the saints, shows for a moment, even to the dullest man, the possibilities of the human race. He has faith, hope, and charity for another being, perhaps but the creation of his imagination; still it is a great advance for a man to be profoundly loving, even in his imagination.

Sir Arthur Helps

Happiness does not lie in happiness, but in the achievement of it.

~

FYODOR DOSTOYEVSKY

I do not ask for any crown
But that which all may win;
Nor try to conquer any world
Except the one within.
Be Thou my guide until I find
Led by a tender hand,
The happy kingdom in myself
And dare to take command.

Louisa May Alcott

For a man to achieve all that is demanded of him he must regard himself as greater than he is.

J. W. von Goethe

I have learnt too much of the heart of man
not to be certain that it is only in the bosom
of my family that I shall find happiness.

~~~

*François Dominique
Toussaint-L'Ouverture*

The ultimate lesson all of us have to
learn is *unconditional love*,
which includes not only others
but ourselves as well.

~ *Elisabeth Kübler-Ross* ~

The trouble with most people is that they think with their hopes or fears or wishes rather than with their minds.

WILL DURANT

I have a lot of things to prove to myself. One is that I can live my life fearlessly.

OPRAH WINFREY

Value friendship for what there is in it, not for what can be gotten out of it.

H. CLAY TRUMBULL

If someone listens, or stretches out a hand,

or whispers a kind word of encouragement, or

attempts to understand a lonely person,

extraordinary things begin to happen.

~

Loretta Girzartis

$\mathcal{Y}$ou have to count on living every single day in a way you believe will make you feel good about your life—so that if it were over tomorrow, you'd be content with yourself.

~~~ ~~~ ~~~

Jane Seymour

$\mathcal{T}$he world will never have lasting peace so long as men reserve for war the finest human qualities. Peace, no less than war, requires idealism and self-sacrifice and a righteous and dynamic faith.

John Foster Dulles

*O*n with the dance, let joy be unconfined" is my motto, whether there's any dance to dance or any joy to unconfine.

Mark Twain

What do we live for, if it is not to make life less difficult for each other?

GEORGE ELIOT

. . . there is a luxury in being quiet in the heart of chaos.

VIRGINIA WOOLF

We learn the inner secret of happiness
when we learn to direct our inner drives, our
interest, and our attention to something
outside ourselves.

Ethel Percy Andrus

*M*y formula for living is quite simple. I get up in the morning and I go to bed at night. In between, I occupy myself as best I can.

Cary Grant

*Nothing is miserable unless
you think it so.*

~

BOETHIUS

*O*nce you can laugh at your own weaknesses, you can move forward. Comedy breaks down walls. It opens up people. If you're good, you can fill up those openings with something positive. Maybe you can combat some of the ugliness in the world.

Goldie Hawn

In a battle of wills, loving kindness is the only weapon that conquers.

VIMALIA McCLURE

I used to trouble about what life was for——now being alive seems sufficient reason.

JOANNA FIELD

Life appears to me too short to be spent in nursing animosity or registering wrong.

CHARLOTTE BRONTË

Take the world as you find it; enjoy everything. "Viva la bagatelle!"

Benjamin Disraeli

The quieter you become, the more you can hear.

—

BABA RAM DASS

*Y*ou are as prone to love as the sun is to shine; it being the most delightful and natural employment of the Soul of Man: without which you are dark and miserable. For certainly he that delights not in Love makes vain the universe, and is of necessity to himself the greatest burden.

Thomas Traherne

It seems to me we can never give up longing

and wishing while we are thoroughly alive.

There are certain things we feel to be beautiful

and good, and we must hunger after them.

George Eliot

*N*otice the world, sense it, react to it, change it. If you work in a room with harsh fluorescent lighting and windows that can't be opened . . . sense how these things present themselves, how they affect you. Don't fall prey to the therapist's fantasy that the problem is always in you, when you're suffering because of the room. Do what you can to change it, make it as personal as you can, fit it to you. Be eccentric; put a lampshade over the light.

Dr. James Hillman

Love is the only force
capable of transforming an
enemy into a friend.

~~~~~

Martin Luther King, Jr.

Trouble is a part of your life, and if you don't share it you don't give the person who loves you enough chance to love you enough.

 Dinah Shore

Whatever you do, put romance and enthusiasm into the life of our children.

~

MARGARET RAMSEY
MACDONALD

*Y*ou live. No use asking whether life will bring you pleasure or unhappiness, whether it will prove a blessing or a curse. Who could answer these questions? You live, you breathe.

George Sand

Develop the art of friendliness. One can experience a variety of emotions staying home and reading or watching television; one will be alive but hardly living. Most of the meaningful aspects of life are closely associated with people. Even the dictionary definition of life involves people.

William L. Abbott

*S*et positive goals and
reasonable expectations.

STEVE STRASSER

Those who would enjoyment gain must find it in the purpose they pursue.

SARAH J. HALE

*T*here is a pleasure

in the pathless woods,

There is a rapture on the lonely shore,

There is a society where none intrudes,

By the deep sea, and music in its roar:

I love not man the less, but nature more.

Lord Byron

If you're worried about that last at bat, you're going to be miserable, you're only going to get depressed, but if you put a picture in your mind that you're going to get a base hit off him the next time, now how do you feel? I try to put positive pictures into the minds of my players.

Tommy Lasorda

To love what you do and feel that it matters—how could anything be more fun?

KATHERINE GRAHAM

A man is happy so long as
he chooses to be happy and
nothing can stop him.

ALEXANDER SOLZHENITSYN

Doing the best at this moment puts you in the best place for the next moment.

❧

OPRAH WINFREY

The supreme happiness of life is the conviction that we are loved.

Victor Hugo

*M*ore and more clearly every day out of biology, anthropology, sociology, history, economic analysis, psychological insight, plain human decency, and common sense, the necessary mandate of survival that we show love of our neighbors as we do ourselves, is being confirmed and reaffirmed.

Ordway Tead

Whatever you attempt, go at it with spirit. Put some in!

DAVID STARR JORDAN

He who plants a tree, he plants love,

Tents of coolness spreading out above

Wayfarers he may not live to see.

Gifts that grow are best.

Lucy Larcom

*C*onfront the dark parts of yourself, and work to banish them with illumination and forgiveness. Your willingness to wrestle with your demons will cause your angels to sing. Use the pain as fuel, as a reminder of your strength.

August Wilson

She knew what all smart women knew: *Laughter* made you live better and longer.

Gail Parent

*I*n spite of all our hopes, dreams, and efforts, change is real and forever. Accept it fearlessly. Investigate the unknown; neither fear nor worship it.

~~~

Joseph A. Bauer

Our happiness in this world depends upon
the affections we are enabled to inspire.

Duchesse de Praslin

I was raised to sense what someone wanted me
to be and be that kind of person. It took me a
long time not to judge myself through someone
else's eyes.

Sally Field

Do not choose for your friends and familiar acquaintances those that are of an estate or quality too much above yours. . . . You will hereby accustom yourselves to live after their rate in clothes, in habit, and in expenses, whereby you will learn a fashion and rank of life above your degree and estate, which will in the end be your undoing.

Sir Matthew Hale

*To understand everything
is to forgive everything.*

~

GAUTAMA BUDDHA

*P*lay so that you may
be serious.

~

*A*NACHARSIS

*F*riendship with oneself is all important,

because without it one cannot be friends with

anyone else in the world.

Eleanor Roosevelt

$\mathcal{D}$on't think! Thinking is the enemy of creativity. It's self-conscious, and anything self-conscious is lousy. You can't *try* to do things. You simply *must* do things.

~ *Ray Bradbury* ~

The emotions may be endless. The more we express them, the more we have to express.

~

E. M. FORSTER

You have freedom when
you're easy in your harness.

❧

ROBERT FROST

All happiness depends on a
leisurely breakfast.

~

JOHN GUNTHER

To have grown wise and kind is real success.

ANONYMOUS

*O*ne is never as fortunate or as

unfortunate as one imagines.

~ *François Duc de La Rochefoucauld* ~

Give me a man who sings at
his work.

＞

THOMAS CARLYLE

To love the beautiful, to desire the good, to do the best.

MOTTO OF *Moses Mendelsohn*

*H*aving only coarse food to eat, plain water to drink, and a bent arm for a pillow, one can still find happiness therein.

 *Confucius*

*W*e can perhaps learn to prepare for love.
We can welcome its coming, we can learn to
treasure and cherish it when it comes, but we
cannot make it happen. We are elected
into love.

Irene Claremont de Castillejo

Suggest what is right, oppose what is wrong; what you think, speak; try to satisfy yourself, and not others; and if you are not popular, you will at least be respected; popularity lasts but a day, respect will descend as a heritage to your children.

T. C. Halliburton

$\mathcal{T}$he human contribution is the essential ingredient. It is only in the giving of oneself to others that we truly live.

Ethel Percy Andrus

*G*rief can take care of itself,
but to get the full value of joy
you must have somebody to
divide it with.

MARK TWAIN

*Each day the world is born
anew
For him who takes it rightly.*

JAMES RUSSELL LOWELL

$\mathcal{I}$f I have been of service, if I have glimpsed

more of the nature and essence of ultimate

good, if I am inspired to reach wider horizons

of thought and action, if I am at peace with

myself, it has been a successful day.

Alex Noble

*T*he real secret of success is enthusiasm. Yes, more than enthusiasm, I would say excitement. I like to see men get excited. When they get excited they make a success of their lives.

Walter Chrysler

Don't be afraid to feel as angry or as loving as you can.

LENA HORNE

*H*appy are they, my son, who shall learn . . . not to despair; but shall remember, that though the day is past, and their strength is wasted, there yet remains one effort to be made; that reformation is never hopeless, nor sincere endeavors ever unassisted; that the wanderer may at length return after all his errors; and that he who implores strength and courage from above, shall find danger and difficulty give way before him.

Samuel Johnson

The bird of paradise alights only upon the hand that does not grasp.

JOHN BERRY

I earn that I eat, get that I wear, owe no man hate, envy no man's happiness; glad of other men's good, content with my harm.

William Shakespeare

If you don't know where you are going, you will probably wind up somewhere else.

❧

DR. LAURENCE J. PETER

$\mathcal{M}$an needs, for his happiness, not only
the enjoyment of this or that, but hope and
enterprise and change.

~ *Bertrand Russell* ~

Take time for all things: great haste makes great waste.

BENJAMIN FRANKLIN

Life begets life. Energy creates energy. It is by spending oneself that one becomes rich.

SARAH BERNHARDT

We must not, in trying to think about how we can make a big difference, ignore the small daily differences we can make which, over time, add up to big differences that we often cannot foresee.

Marian Wright Edelman

$\mathcal{N}$o man ever sank under the burden of the day. It is when tomorrow's burden is added to the burden of today that the weight is more than a man can bear. Never load yourself so. If you find yourself so loaded, at least remember this: it is your own doing, not God's. He begs you to leave the future to Him, and mind the present.

George Macdonald

*Y*ou must have long-range goals
to keep you from being frustrated
by short-range failures.

CHARLES C. NOBLE

*I*t is a curious thought, but it is only when you see people looking ridiculous, that you realize just how much you love them.

~ *Agatha Christie* ~

The unexamined life is not worth living.

*P*LATO

Do not say, "It is morning," and dismiss it with a name of yesterday. See it for the first time as a newborn child that has no name.

Rabindranath Tagore

Nothing will content him who is not content with a little.

GREEK PROVERB

*T*ake time to work—it is the price of success;
Take time to think—it is the source of power;
Take time to play—it is the secret of perpetual youth;
Take time to read—it is the foundation of wisdom;
Take time to worship—it is the highway to reverence;
Take time to be friendly—it is the road to happiness;
Take time to dream—it is hitching our wagon to a star;
Take time to love and be loved—it is the privilege
   of the gods.

Anonymous

$\mathcal{I}$f you don't daydream and kind of plan things out in your imagination, you never get there. So you have to start someplace.

Robert Duvall

$\mathcal{T}$he purpose of life is living. Men and women should get the most they can out of their lives. The smallest, the tiniest intellect may be quite as valuable to itself; it may have all the capacity for enjoyment that the wisest has.

Clarence Darrow

A house is a home when it
shelters the body and comforts
the soul.

~

PHILLIP MOFFITT

Just the knowledge that a good book is
waiting one at the end of a long day makes
that day happier.

~~ *Kathleen Norris* ~~

*S*ooner or later we all discover that the important moments in life are not the advertised ones, not the birthdays, the graduations, the weddings, not the great goals achieved. The real milestones are less prepossessing. They come to the door of memory unannounced, stray dogs that amble in, sniff around a bit, and simply never leave. Our lives are measured by these.

Susan B. Anthony

Life appears to me too short to be spent in nursing animosity or registering wrongs.

CHARLOTTE BRONTË

*T*o live happily with other
people, ask of them only what
they can give.

TRISTAN BERNARD

Good friends, good books and a sleepy conscience: this is the ideal life.

MARK TWAIN

*L*ove of humanity tends readily to become abstract, to exist in fancy rather than in reality. Love needs to be concentrated on specific objects. One cannot love all men equally. We choose, and we ought to choose the objects of our love. Love, humanity, must be positive. People often take the hatred of another nation to be the love of one's own. It is far higher to feel no hatred, but to love positively.

Tomás G. Masaryk

*Do not make yourself low;
people will tread on your head.*

~

YIDDISH PROVERB

$\mathcal{W}$e must overcome the notion that we must be regular. It robs us of the chance to be extraordinary and leads us to the mediocre.

～ *Uta Hagen* ～

One word frees us of all the weight and pain of life: That word is love.

Sophocles

The only way to make a man trustworthy is to trust him.

HENRY L. STIMSON

One hour of downright love is
worth an hour of dully living on.

APHRA BEHN

We are the hero of our
own story.

MARY McCARTHY

*I*f you approach each new person you meet in a spirit of adventure, you will find yourself endlessly fascinated by the new channels of thought and experience and personality that you encounter. I do not mean simply the famous people of the world, but people from every walk and condition of life.

Eleanor Roosevelt

Accept things as they are, not as you wish them to be.

NAPOLEON I

$\mathcal{L}$ove is not self-sacrifice, but the most profound assertion of your own needs and values. It is for your *own* happiness that you need the person you love, and that is the greatest compliment, the greatest tribute you can pay to that person.

Ayn Rand

*I*ntegrate what you believe into every single area of your life. Take your heart to work and ask the most and best of everybody else. Don't let your special character and values, the secret that you know and no one else does, the truth—don't let that get swallowed up by the great chewing complacency.

Meryl Streep

If the world seems cold to you,
kindle fires to warm it.

LUCY LARCOM

*O*f course there is no formula for success
except, perhaps, an unconditional acceptance
of life and what it brings.

Arthur Rubinstein

A good marriage is that in which each appoints the other the guardian of his solitude.

RAINER MARIA RILKE

*L*ove does not die easily. It is a living thing. It thrives in the face of all life's hazards, save one—neglect.

James D. Bryden

Let me listen to me and not to them.

GERTRUDE STEIN

*I*f we don't change, we don't grow. If we don't grow, we are not really living.

~ *Gail Sheehy* ~

It is astonishing how little one feels poverty when one loves.

JOHN BULWER

The cure for all the ills and wrongs, the cares, the sorrows, and the crimes of humanity, all lie in the one word "love." It is the divine vitality that everywhere produces and restores life. To each and every one of us, it gives the power of working miracles.

Lydia M. Child

*Y*ou don't have to be afraid of change. You don't have to worry about what's been taken *away*. Just look to see what's been *added*.

Jackie Greer

$\mathcal{L}$earn the wisdom of compromise, for it is better to bend a little than to break.

⟿ *Jane Wells* ⟿

To live happily is an inward power of the soul.

~

MARCUS AURELIUS

*K*eep the other person's well-being in mind
when you feel an attack of soul-purging truth
coming on.

~

Betty White

$\mathcal{Y}$our best shot at happiness, self-worth, and personal satisfaction—the things that constitute real success—is not in learning as much as you can but in performing as well as you can something that you consider worthwhile. Whether that is healing the sick, giving hope to the hopeless, adding to the beauty of the world, or saving the world from nuclear holocaust . . .

William Raspberry

One must never look for happiness: one meets it by the way. . . .

ISABELLE EBERHARDT

*L*ove is a symbol of eternity. It wipes out all
sense of time, destroying all memory of a
beginning and all fear of an end.

❧

Madame de Staël

The great pleasure in life is
doing what people say you
cannot do.

❧

WALTER BAGEHOT

I really believe that if you know what you're doing, if you believe in what you're doing, you can make it—in any business.

Reva Yares

*S*ometimes a life, like a house, needs renovating, the smell of new wood, new rooms in the heart, unimagined until one begins the work. One rebuilds because the structure deserves a renewing.

~ Doris Schwerin ~

$\mathcal{W}$hen your schedule leaves you brain-drained and stressed to exhaustion, it's time to give up something. Delegate. Say no. Be brutal. It's like cleaning out a closet—after a while, it gets easier to get rid of things. You discover that you really didn't need them anyway.

Marilyn Ruman

There is no beautifier of complexion,
or form, or behavior, like the wish to
scatter joy and not pain around us.

Ralph Waldo Emerson

I believe if a man sets an attainable goal
for himself and works to attain it, conscious that
when he does so he will then set another goal
for himself, he will have a full, busy, and—
for this reason—a happy life.

Lionel Barrymore

*M*y crown is in my heart, not on my head;
not deck'd with diamonds and Indian stones,
nor to be seen: my crown is call'd content;
a crown it is that seldom kings enjoy.

William Shakespeare

*H*appiness is a by-product of an effort to make someone else happy.

~ *Gretta Palmer* ~

It is by believing, hoping, loving, and doing that man finds joy and peace.

JOHN LANCASTER SPALDING

Wisdom is a tree of life to those who eat her fruit; happy is the man who keeps on eating it.

Proverbs 3:18

This book was typeset in Centaur MT and

Savoye Script, by Caitlin Daniels

and Judith Stagnitto Abbate.

Book design by Judith Stagnitto Abbate